Steam Destinati
Bournemouth

Colourpoint Books

Tom Heavyside

Steam Destination Bournemouth

6 5 4 3 2 1

© Tom Heavyside and Colourpoint Books 2006

Designed by Colourpoint Books, Newtownards
Printed by: W&G Baird Ltd

ISBN 1 904242 67 7
     978 1 904242 67 3

Colourpoint Books
Colourpoint House
Jubilee Business Park
21 Jubilee Road
Newtownards
County Down
Northern Ireland
BT23 4YH
Tel: 028 9182 0505
Fax: 028 9182 1900
E-mail: info@colourpoint.co.uk
Web-site: www.colourpoint.co.uk

Lancashire man Tom Heavyside was first introduced to the delights and idiosyncrasies of Southern Region steam during family holidays spent at Bournemouth in the mid-1950s. He very quickly realised that there was much more of interest at Bournemouth Central station and on day trips to such places as Eastleigh and Salisbury, rather than whiling away the time on the beach or exploring the various chines. During the 1960s, as steam gradually retreated from the lines in the south, he grasped every available opportunity to imbibe Southern steam, as on various expeditions to the capital when visits to Waterloo station and Nine Elms shed were always on the list of priorities. Further, he has always had a particular fascination for the Bulleid Pacifics, both in their original form and as rebuilt. He still enjoys the sight and sound of former Southern Region locomotives on occasional visits to preserved lines such as the Bluebell, Mid-Hants and Swanage railways, while pleasingly, in more recent times, a few examples have been found permanent homes much nearer to his Lancashire home.

All photographs are by the author.

Front cover: The classic view of Bournemouth Central station. Here the doyen of the 110-strong 'West Country/Battle of Britain' class 4-6-2s, No 34001 *Exeter*, in its modified form as rebuilt at Eastleigh Works in November 1957, departs with a train for London Waterloo on 8 September 1962. The Pacific first saw the light of day at Brighton Works in May 1945, although it was the next month before it entered revenue earning service when it looked very different shrouded in an air-smoothed casing. The Bulleid Pacifics, both the 'WC/BBs' and the slightly larger and heavier 'Merchant Navies' introduced four years earlier, were very familiar sights at Bournemouth right up until the demise of steam in southern England in July 1967.

Rear cover: During our journey west from Waterloo to Bournemouth, we also squeeze in a visit to the Isle of Wight to witness some vintage motive power at work. On what was a rather damp 25 May 1966, the elder statesman, class O2 0-4-4T No W14 *Fishbourne*, built at the London and South Western Railway's works at Nine Elms in December 1889 as their No 178, is seen leaving Ryde St John's Road with the 13.19 Ryde Pier Head to Shanklin service. The locomotive had been on the island since 1936. On the right coaching stock is stabled on the down loop line with the roof of Ryde Works in the background.

Introduction

The former London and South Western Railway main line from Waterloo to Bournemouth, and on to Weymouth, had the dubious distinction of being the last preserve of regular steam-operated passenger services in and out of the capital. It was, in fact, quite late in the day in the history of steam on Britain's railways before diesel and electric traction took full command of the services along this route, the iron horse finally bowing out on Sunday 9 July 1967. During the last years of steam the line naturally attracted a great deal of attention from the railway enthusiast fraternity. Similarly, many took the opportunity to take a trip across The Solent to the Isle of Wight, where steam reigned virtually unchallenged until the last day of 1966.

Looking back to the beginning of the railway era, the eastern section of what later became the main line from the capital to the south-west corner of Hampshire and on into Dorset was promoted by the London and Southampton Railway, the first stage from Nine Elms (London) to Woking being opened in May 1838. By the time it became possible to travel through to Southampton in May 1840, the company had already changed its name to the London and South Western Railway (LSWR), a title much more appropriate to its long-term aspirations which stretched far beyond its initial London to Southampton corridor. At the London end the line was extended from Nine Elms to Waterloo, a terminus much more conveniently situated for the City, in July 1848.

West of Southampton the first development was the opening of the Southampton and Dorchester Railway (SDR) in August 1847, which traced a rather roundabout route via Brockenhurst, Ringwood and Wimborne, a line often referred to as 'Castleman's Corkscrew' after the Wimborne solicitor who was the main instigator behind the scheme. In time, a branch south from Ringwood was promoted by the Ringwood, Christchurch and Bournemouth Railway (RCBR), which commenced operating

as far as Christchurch in November 1862, with the extension to Bournemouth East not completed until March 1870. Both the aforementioned companies were destined to become part of the London and South Western Railway empire, the SDR in 1848 and the RCBR in 1874.

The remaining pieces of what eventually became the main line from London to Bournemouth as we know it today were laid by the LSWR. First, a short spur was put down at Northam in 1858 so as to facilitate through running to and from the west without the inconvenience of having to reverse at the first Southampton station (later to be known as Southampton Terminus). However, it was another twenty-seven years, in July 1885, before passengers were able to continue beyond Bournemouth East station to what later became known as Bournemouth Central, with the option of travelling even further west into Dorset. Finally, the direct line from Christchurch to Brockenhurst via New Milton and Sway was opened in March 1888.

A later decision by the LSWR, in December 1912, proved one of the most far-reaching ever by a British railway company when it chose to convert some of its London suburban services to electric traction, not by stringing out miles of overhead cabling as had the neighbouring London, Brighton and South Coast Railway (LBSCR) but by the far simpler expedient of laying an extra third rail to carry the current. The first LSWR electric trains were introduced between Waterloo and Wimbledon via Clapham Junction and East Putney in October 1915.

The Grouping of the railways in 1923 brought the lines formerly owned by the LSWR under the control of the newly-formed Southern Railway, which opted to extend the electrified third rails even further across its territory, in the process dismantling the LBSCR-erected overhead catenary in favour of the LSWR system. By 1937 the long tentacles of conductor rails had reached out from Waterloo to, among other places, Pirbright Junction, west of Brookwood, where they branched off from the main line in the direction of Alton. West of Pirbright, and on to Basingstoke and the south-west, steam remained in sole command.

Later, under the 1955 British Railways Modernisation Plan, it was envisaged that the Bournemouth main line would be dieselised, but after much deliberation the BR Board had a complete change of heart and instead settled for the well-proven ideals of its predecessors by agreeing to extend the live 750V dc conductor rails beyond Pirbright through to the burgeoning Hampshire town (later to become part of Dorset). It was September 1964 before the decision was made public with completion planned for the summer of 1967. Meanwhile, in the interim, and to the joy of many, steam would perforce have to remain as the mainstay of the motive power department, although in the event, due to the run-down state of many of the locomotives, from late 1966 a few diesels had to be borrowed from the Western Region to bolster the flagging steam stock.

A little earlier, at the turn of the decade into the 1960s, the Southern Region had had over 1,100 steam locomotives on its books, including some that were quite elderly. As the 1960s progressed, as elsewhere, numbers rapidly diminished, so that by January 1966 only 226 were listed in capital stock, 212 serving the lines out of Waterloo to Weymouth and Salisbury along with various offshoots, and 14 on the Isle of Wight. In respect of those on the mainland, 89 had either been handed down to BR by the Southern Railway when the railways became state-owned in January 1948, or had been built to their drawings in the years immediately following nationalisation. BR Standard designs accounted for 110 locomotives, some having been imported from other Regions after becoming redundant at their previous sheds. The remaining 13 were Ivatt LMS class 2MT 2-6-2Ts, eight built at Crewe Works in the early 1950s as part of a batch ordered specifically for the Southern Region, the other five having been employed on their native London Midland Region before migrating south.

Across on the Isle of Wight at the start of 1966 the surviving sections of the once-extensive rail network represented a veritable time warp. The 14 engines on the stock list, all ex-LSWR class O2 0-4-4Ts, were by far the oldest engines in day-to-day use still hauling passenger trains, having emanated from Nine Elms Works back in the early 1890s, while the coaching stock was of either London, Brighton and South Coast Railway or South Eastern and Chatham Railway origin. The status quo was maintained until the end of the year when the last remaining passenger service, that from Ryde to Shanklin, was temporarily withdrawn pending the introduction of some electric-powered former London Transport tube stock the following March.

At the dawn of 1967, the mainland Southern sheds had 120 steam locomotives available for traffic. Except for the last few N and U class Moguls and Q1 class 0-6-0s which had been disposed of during 1966, the remaining classes which had started the previous year were still represented, with the Bulleid Pacifics, 46 in total, still well to the fore. Somewhat amazingly, in March 1966 the stock had been supplemented by an engine of a class hitherto unknown on the Southern Region, BR Standard 3MT 2-6-0 No 77014. In earlier years the 20 members of this class, built at Swindon in 1954, had confined their activities to the North Eastern and Scottish regions, that is until November 1964 when Nos 77011 and 77014 were transferred across the Pennines from Stourton shed (Leeds) to Northwich. When the pair became surplus at this Cheshire outpost in the winter of 1966, the former was withdrawn while No 77014 was sent south to Guildford, where it became something of a celebrity. Meanwhile, on the Isle of Wight two O2s were maintained for a few weeks purely to assist the engineering department in preparing the ground for the replacement electric service.

As the months of 1967 passed, so the number of steam locomotive diagrams became less and less. Even so, 78 steam locomotives managed to cling on to life into July, although by then many were simply spending most of their time resting in the sheds. Sunday 9 July was to prove the final day for the iron horse, but to the disappointment of many, that day there was to be no last fling out of Waterloo during the hours of daylight (the Southern Region official farewell specials had run the previous Sunday), the nocturnal 02.30 to Poole being the ultimate passenger train to pass through the London suburbs in the down direction with steam at the head. Later in the day two steam-hauled trains finished their journeys at Waterloo. First 'West Country' Pacific No 34021 *Dartmoor* arrived during the early afternoon with a boat train from Southampton, while the very last BR scheduled steam-hauled train to enter this spacious terminal, the 14.07 from Weymouth, was hauled by 'Merchant Navy' 4-6-2 No 35030 *Elder Dempster Lines*. Ironically, the lot fell to the relative newcomer to the area, No 77014, to perform the last rites on the Southern Region, when it took charge of the 20.50 van train from Bournemouth to Weymouth. The next day, sadly, the long-familiar sounds of steam were nowhere to be heard across southern England.

Through the pages of this volume we turn the clock back to the 1960s and relive a leisurely journey down the line from Waterloo to the Hampshire coast as experienced in the days of steam. En route, after passing through the London commuter belt, the important railway town of Eastleigh and the maritime port of Southampton, as we pass through the New Forest the opportunity is taken to make a brief detour along the last steam-worked branch on British Railways, that from Brockenhurst to Lymington, in order to cross The Solent to the Isle of Wight, before we continue west to our ultimate destination – the popular holiday resort of Bournemouth. For those who had the opportunity to experience steam during its final years along this former LSWR main line, it really was a glorious era. It was certainly one to be savoured.

Selected References:

Bird, John H, *Southern Steam Sunset*, Runpast Publishing, 1997

Bradley, DL, *Locomotives of the London & South Western Railway Part 2*, Railway Correspondence and Travel Society, 1967

Bradley, DL, *Locomotives of the Southern Railway Part 2*, Railway Correspondence and Travel Society, 1976

Freeman Allen, G, *The Southern Since 1948*, Ian Allan, 1987

Hawkins, Chris and Reeve, George, *An Historical Survey of Southern Sheds*, Oxford Publishing Co, 1979

Kichenside, GM, *Isle of Wight Album*, Ian Allan, 1967

Mitchell, Vic and Smith, Keith, *Waterloo to Woking, Woking to Southampton, Southampton to Bournemouth including the Fawley and Lymington Branches*, Middleton Press, 1986, 1988, 1987

Nock, OS, *The London & South Western Railway*, Ian Allan, 1966

White, HP, *A Regional History of the Railways of Great Britain, Volume 2 Southern England*, David & Charles, 1982

Acknowledgements:

I am much indebted to Paul Abell, John Fozard, Ron Simpson and Mike Thompson for their help during the compilation of this volume. I would like to thank too, even at this late stage, the BR Southern Region personnel who granted permits on numerous occasions during the 1960s to enable visits to the various engine sheds and Eastleigh locomotive works, not forgetting the staff on the ground who I seem to remember were always most welcoming. Forty years on it is all still very much appreciated.

Route maps

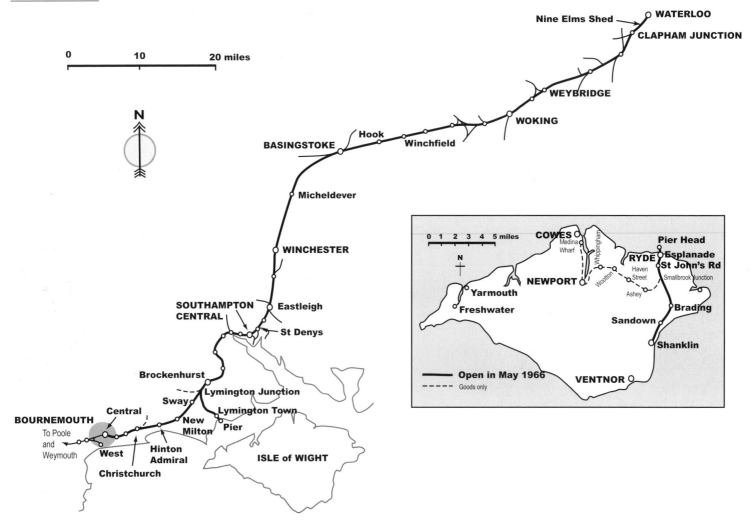

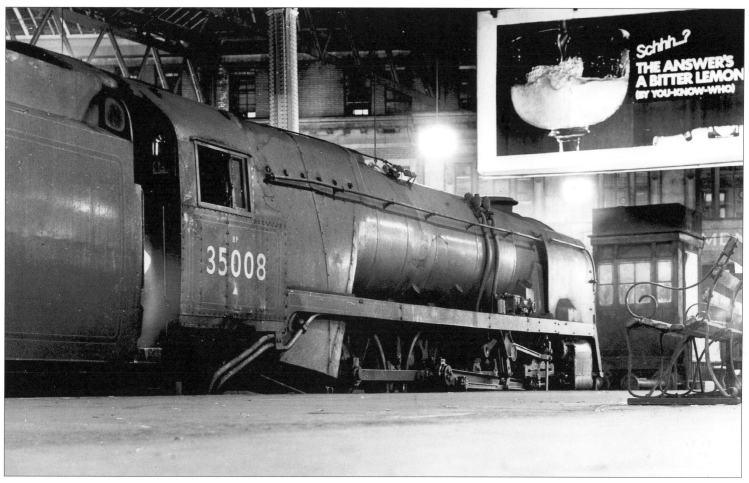

A scene witnessed at Waterloo station by countless numbers of passengers over the years, a steam locomotive standing close to the buffer stops after entering the station with a train from the west. This is rebuilt 'Merchant Navy' class 4-6-2 No 35008, devoid of its *Orient Line* nameplates, after bringing in the 17.30 from Weymouth on Friday 12 May 1967. Overhead an advertisement for a well-known drink product also vies for attention. The Pacific was trapped in this position until such time that one of the station pilots was able to remove the empty coaching stock to the sidings at Clapham Junction for servicing. Just over eight weeks later, on Sunday 9 July 1967, this scenario was re-enacted for the very last time following the arrival of fellow 'Merchant Navy' No 35030 *Elder Dempster Lines* at the head of the 14.07 from Weymouth, with the poignant inscription 'Last Steam, Grand Finale Weymouth to Waterloo 9-7-67' chalked on its smokebox door. The 30 members of this class, built at Eastleigh during the years 1941 to 1949, were all rebuilt in the same workshops between February 1956 and October 1959 when the air-smoothed casing and the chain-driven valve gear in an enclosed oil bath were dispensed with, the modified design having a much more conventional appearance. No 35008 emerged from Eastleigh Works in its new guise in May 1957 and when withdrawn in July 1967 had covered 1,286,418 miles, only No 35007 *Aberdeen Commonwealth* recording a higher mileage.

During the last weeks of steam at Waterloo, station pilot duties were often in the hands of the 1952-introduced BR Standard class 3MT 2-6-2Ts and some of the class 2MT 2-6-2Ts built to a LMS pattern dating from 1946. Nearest the camera on 13 May 1967 is one of the former, No 82019, constructed at Swindon Works in 1952 for the Southern Region. It worked from Redhill, Exmouth Junction and Eastleigh sheds before being transferred to Nine Elms during autumn 1962. Behind is Crewe Works 1951-built No 41298. Despite its LMS pedigree this was always a Southern Region engine, having spells at Bricklayers Arms (London), Barnstaple Junction and Weymouth sheds before a final move to Nine Elms brought it back to the capital in the autumn of 1966. Both engines were last used at Waterloo on the penultimate day of steam traction, Saturday 8 July 1967, and while No 82019 was broken up a few months later by Bird's in their scrapyard at Risca, near Newport, No 41298 was preserved and can be seen today at the Buckinghamshire Railway Centre at Quainton Road, near Aylesbury.

On the same day, rebuilt 'West Country' class Pacific No 34008 *Padstow* edges away from Waterloo with a special boat train working bound for Southampton Docks in connection with a P&O sailing, the leading vehicle no doubt crammed with items of luggage. Soon after the start of its career the engine travelled to Padstow, to what was once the far extremity of the London and South Western Railway's domain on the north Cornwall coast, to be formally named by the Chairman of the local Urban District Council on 31 October 1945. Regrettably, by May 1967 the nameplates, along with the accompanying county coat of arms, had been removed, although the backing plates were still in position. On the left is one of the versatile electro-diesel locomotives, No E6008 (later No 73102) built by English Electric at their Vulcan Foundry works at Newton-le-Willows in Lancashire in October 1965.

Two miles down the line from Waterloo was the former LSWR motive power depot at Nine Elms, coded 70A in BR days. It was a massive shed, in its final form having 25 roads. In earlier times it had had up to 200 locomotives on its books, but by the summer of 1950 the total had been reduced to 99. Simmering in the shed yard, amidst some rather untidy heaps of ash and clinker, on 7 October 1965, prepared and ready to back down to Waterloo, is 'Merchant Navy' Pacific No 35022 *Holland-America Line* from Weymouth shed. That afternoon (a Thursday) the shed hosted 61 engines, consisting of five 'Merchant Navy' and 27 'West Country/Battle of Britain' Pacifics, U class

2-6-0 No 31809 and two of the rather ungainly Q1 class 0-6-0s Nos 33009 and 33026, together with 26 BR Standards. The latter were made up of eleven class 5MT 4-6-0s, two class 4MT 4-6-0s, one class 4MT 2-6-0 No 76066, two class 4MT 2-6-4Ts and ten class 3MT 2-6-2Ts. Sad to relate, seven of the engines had in fact already been withdrawn – 'Merchant Navy' No 35019 *French Line C.G.T.*, 'West Countries' Nos 34007 *Wadebridge* (only that very day) and 34042 *Dorchester*, Q1 No 33009, BR Standard class 5MT No 73112 *Morgan le Fay* (after less than ten years service) and Standard 3MT 2-6-2Ts Nos 82005 and 82020.

Looking almost forlorn at Nine Elms shed on 13 May 1967, with the 400 ton-capacity coaling plant towering overhead, is class 2MT 2-6-2T No 41312. Constructed to a design by HG Ivatt for the LMS, No 41312 was outshopped from Crewe Works in May 1952 as part of an order for the Southern Region. It was employed by the sheds at Faversham, Ashford, Barnstaple Junction and Brighton before it was moved to Bournemouth in May 1964. While at the latter it had the dubious distinction of heading the last steam services along the Lymington branch on Sunday 2 April 1967 before ending its BR days at Nine Elms. It was then sold to Woodham Bros at Barry in South Wales where it lay derelict for over six and a half years before being rescued for preservation in August 1974. In recent times it has seen service on a number of heritage railways.

Resting inside Nine Elms shed on 13 May 1967 is Bulleid 'West Country' Pacific No 34023 *Blackmore Vale*, one of only two still clothed in the distinctive air-smoothed casing to survive until the very end of Southern Region steam – the other was No 34102 *Lapford*. Notice, too, the Boxpok wheels as developed by Bulleid in conjunction with Firth-Brown's, a steel company based in Sheffield. *Blackmore Vale* first left Brighton Works in February 1946 as No 21C123 with the name spelt Blackmoor Vale. The numbering system was Bulleid's unorthodox method of identifying his engines, the letter C indicating the number of coupled axles and the first two digits the leading and trailing axles. It received its BR number in April 1948 and the name was amended in April 1950. During its twenty-one-year main line career it travelled over 920,000 miles, having spells working from Ramsgate, Nine Elms, Salisbury, Exmouth Junction and Eastleigh sheds, before moving to Nine Elms for a second time in April 1967. After being rendered obsolete three months later, *Blackmore Vale* was purchased from BR for preservation and is now among 20 of the class still in existence. For the past thirty years it has been accumulating yet more mileage on the Bluebell Railway which runs north from Sheffield Park in East Sussex, presently running in its original guise as No 21C123.

One of the rebuilt 'Battle of Britain' class Pacifics No 34052 *Lord Dowding*, similar in all but name to the 'West Country' class, passes the electricity sub-station at Weybridge, 19 miles from Waterloo, with a train destined for Salisbury on 12 May 1967. *Lord Dowding* was released into traffic from Brighton Works on the last day of 1946 and apart from spending fourteen months at Nine Elms from February 1950, followed by two months at Exmouth Junction, was otherwise only ever attached to Salisbury shed. It was rebuilt at Eastleigh in September 1958. This 3-cylinder class, after the maximum boiler pressure had been reduced from 280lbs to 250lbs per square inch, had a nominal tractive effort of 27,715lbs. In 1961 the BR power classification was amended to 7P6F from 7P5F. As far as the main route to the west is concerned, Weybridge station, seen in the background, only has platform faces by the outer slow lines. The tracks bearing off to the left provide a longer and much slower alternative route to Waterloo via Staines (where a change is necessary) and Richmond, the branch services using the bay platform to the left of the up slow line. The 68-lever signal box controlling trains along this section can be seen above the sixth carriage. It was decommissioned in March 1970 when its functions were taken over by Surbiton Power Box.

During the same afternoon as the picture overleaf, approaching Weybridge from the opposite direction and running under clear signals, is Nine Elms-allocated 'Merchant Navy' 4-6-2 No 35003 *Royal Mail* heading for the capital with a Channel Islands boat express from Weymouth. It has just overtaken an electric multiple-unit on the up slow line. Like the 'WC/BB' boilers, those fitted to the 'Merchant Navies' were originally pressed to 280lbs per square inch giving the class a tractive effort of 37,515lbs, but after they too had had their safety valves adjusted so that they released any excess steam once the pressure had reached 250lbs, tractive effort was reduced to 33,495lbs. They had a power classification of 8P. At the time *Royal Mail* was the oldest 'Merchant Navy' on the books of BR, as it had been since November 1964 when class leader No 35001 *Channel Packet* was taken out of service, the second engine to roll off the assembly lines at Eastleigh, No 35002 *Union Castle*, having been withdrawn the previous February. No 35003 as No 21C3 first saw the light of day in September 1941, having spent most of the intervening period (nearly twenty-two years from the autumn of 1942) on the books of Exmouth Junction shed. It was rebuilt at Eastleigh in August 1959, prior to which it had recorded 859,784 miles, with a further 272,009 being added afterwards, to give a final figure in July 1967 of 1,131,793 miles.

Named after a former General Manager of the Southern Railway, rebuilt 'Battle of Britain' class Pacific No 34090 *Sir Eustace Missenden, Southern Railway* hurries through Winchfield and under a quite magnificent signal gantry with the 17.30 from Waterloo to Bournemouth on 23 May 1966. Note the co-acting home signals set at different heights to assist sighting, and the mineral wagons in the goods yard on the right. The position of the signals and points were altered by a low-pressure pneumatic system as part of a scheme installed by the LSWR between Woking and Basingstoke during the early years of the twentieth century, the route being quadrupled at the same time. The original arms were lower quadrants with the sections between stations working automatically. The signal box at Winchfield can be seen behind the gantry on the island platform between the up and down fast lines. The air pressure method required smaller frames in the signal boxes than was the case with more conventional methods, since some levers were able to operate more than one function, that at Winchfield having 36 working examples plus another 12 which were spare. The third rail required for the forthcoming electrification is already in place alongside three of the tracks through the station, but has still to be laid by the down slow in the foreground on the right. During the modernisation process the semaphores were all swept away in favour of multiple-aspect colour-light signals, those installed at Winchfield being controlled from a new power box opened at Basingstoke the following November.

Derby Works October 1951-built BR Standard class 5MT 4-6-0 No 73020 guides its eleven-coach train towards Hook station while en route to the capital from Bournemouth on 23 May 1966. This engine had a rather varied career being based at Chester Midland, Willesden, Chester Midland again, Chester West, Shrewsbury and Swindon sheds before settling at Weymouth in September 1958. It remained at the Dorset coast shed until it was moved to Guildford in April 1967 and was last reported in use on Saturday 8 July of that year when it had charge of a late afternoon empty stock train bound for Weymouth, whereupon the fire was dropped for the last time. It was subsequently consigned to oblivion by the South Wales scrap merchant John Cashmore Ltd of Newport in January 1968.

The down 'Bournemouth Belle' Pullman train, the 12.30 from Waterloo, due to arrive at the Hampshire resort at 14.45, nears Basingstoke behind rebuilt 'West Country' Pacific No 34021 *Dartmoor* on 26 May 1966. If normal custom was adhered to *Dartmoor* would return the Pullman cars to London later in the afternoon. This prestigious service was introduced by the Southern Railway in July 1931, passengers paying a supplement in order to enjoy the extravagances of its plush interior. In earlier years the locomotive normally carried a large oblong headboard in front of the smokebox door in keeping with the status of the train, but regrettably this was often left behind at the shed during the closing months of steam.

On the same day as the previous photograph, Nine Elms-allocated unmodified 'West Country' No 34038 *Lynton* threads its way through the complex of lines and sidings at Basingstoke as it heads for home with a lengthy parcels train from Southampton. The engine is still sporting the 'Statesman' headboard from its previous task – a boat train from Waterloo to Southampton Docks in connection with an ocean liner sailing. On the left, by the east signal box, known as 'A' box in later years, a diesel shunter goes about its business while the station is visible beyond. Above the third and fourth vans is the still to be fitted out Basingstoke power signal box which was commissioned the following November. Behind the embankment on the right is the former Great Western Railway route to Reading and the north. No 34038, built at Brighton in 1946, took its name from the north Devon coastal town of Lynton. In its early days it was based at Stewarts Lane and Brighton sheds prior to a move to the West Country in the spring of 1951 where it was assigned to Plymouth Friary and Exmouth Junction sheds. During the autumn of 1960 it went back to Brighton, while a year later it was relocated to Eastleigh before a final move to Nine Elms at the beginning of 1965.

The driver of rebuilt 'West Country' 4-6-2 No 34025 *Whimple*, in charge of a Waterloo to Salisbury service, pulls the bag away from the tender after topping it up with water at Basingstoke on 24 May 1966. The train will diverge from the Bournemouth route 2½ miles further west, at Worting Junction and then pass under Battledown flyover which carries the up Bournemouth line overhead. On the left is Basingstoke West signal box, while hidden from view on the right is the three-road Basingstoke shed, coded 70D until September 1963 when its allocation was dispersed, although it continued to be used as a stabling and signing-on point until the end of steam in July 1967. The locomotive carried the nameplates *Rough Tor* for a period of just twelve days during April 1948 before they were quickly replaced the next month by the *Whimple* plates. It was among the first batch of the class to be rebuilt at Eastleigh Works, re-entering traffic in the form seen here in October 1957, four months after the first to be modified, No 34005 *Barnstaple*, had lost its air-smoothed casing.

During the last week in April 1966, the island platform at Micheldever was reinstated after lying derelict for many years. At the same time, at what is the only station on the 19-mile stretch between Basingstoke and Winchester, the former up and down loop lines and their adjacent platforms were abandoned. The redundant rails and sleepers were quickly removed. As the author stands on the old down platform 'West Country'

Pacific No 34038 *Lynton* rushes through on its way to Bournemouth on 23 May 1966. The locomotive was condemned three weeks later and despatched shortly afterwards to John Cashmore's yard at Newport for breaking. Later in the year, during November, the characterful former LSWR signal box suffered a similar fate when its responsibilities passed to the new power box at Eastleigh.

Earlier that morning Eastleigh-based rebuilt 'Battle of Britain' Pacific No 34090 *Sir Eustace Missenden, Southern Railway* was captured on film passing Micheldever heading for the capital, the fireman no doubt feeling relieved that there is only another two miles of climbing before the summit of the long 21-mile incline from St Denys, much of it at 1-in-252, is reached at Litchfield Tunnel. In the foreground the trackbed of the recently-lifted former down slow line can be clearly seen. No 34090 was seen again later in the day at Winchfield as depicted on page 15. The original ownership of the route is evident from the sign at the end of the platform, with just the letters 'S' and 'R' on the top line being highlighted so as to emphasise its continuing relevance that "Passengers Must Cross Line By Subway", the characters 'L', '&' and 'W' only being noticeable on close examination. The locomotive was completed at Brighton Works under the auspices of British Railways in February 1949 and was rebuilt at Eastleigh in August 1960. In its original condition it ran 444,011 miles, with a final tally of 743,948 miles when retired from service in July 1967. Interestingly, the leading carriage on the train is an early example of BR Mark 2 stock, a type still in service today. This example is a side corridor First, in SR green.

The last in sequence of the 172 BR Standard class 5MT 4-6-0s built between 1951 and 1957, No 73171, sprints through the cathedral city of Winchester with a boat train from Southampton Docks, as a 'Hampshire' diesel multiple-unit slows for the station stop with a down local on 26 May 1966. The station itself is obscured by the drifting steam from No 73171, as almost is the one-road corrugated-iron engine shed, a sub-depot of Eastleigh, in the tightly-curved up goods yard on the right. For many years the shed was home to an ex-LSWR class B4 0-4-0T (see page 30). It was usurped by a diesel shunter in October 1963. In the left foreground the cattle pens and adjacent loading dock appear not to have been used for some time. New from Doncaster Works in May 1957, No 73171 was not in fact the last of the class to take to the rails, that distinction befalling No 73154 which appeared from Derby Works the following month. For the first few years of its short life No 73171 was domiciled on the North Eastern Region at York, Leeds Holbeck and Royston (near Barnsley) sheds, before transferring its allegiance to the Southern Region in September 1963. On moving to more warmer climes it went first to Feltham shed and then in November 1964 to Eastleigh. It was deleted from capital stock in October 1966.

With the station clocks showing 9.38, passengers waiting under the canopy on the up platform at Winchester City prepare to board a Bournemouth to Waterloo semi-fast service on the sunny morning of 27 May 1966. In charge is 'Merchant Navy' class 4-6-2 No 35003 *Royal Mail*, allocated at the time to Bournemouth shed where it had been based since September 1964. In October 1966 it moved to Weymouth before finally ending its days attached to Nine Elms from April 1967. The appendage City was added to the station name by BR on 26 September 1949 to distinguish it from the former Didcot, Newbury and Southampton Railway (Great Western Railway from 1923) station which from the same date was given the suffix Chesil, having previously been known as Winchester Cheesehill. After steam had finished, from the timetable instigated on 10 July 1967 the ex-LSWR station reverted to plain Winchester, Chesil having closed its doors permanently after the last train had departed on Saturday 9 September 1961.

Derby Works 1955-built BR Standard class 5MT 4-6-0 No 73088 *Joyous Gard* from Guildford shed passes Winchester with a short parcels train heading towards Southampton on Sunday 22 May 1966. The colour-light signal at the end of the down platform stands ready to replace the adjacent semaphore in the autumn. The platforms had only been extended the previous year, severing the direct connection from the south into the goods yard. No 73088 was honoured with its name while based at Nine Elms in May 1961, following the decision by the Southern Region in 1959 to distinguish twenty of this class by reusing names that had previously adorned Urie 'King Arthur' class 4-6-0s, this particular name having formerly graced No 30741 before it was taken out of service in February 1956. The 'second' *Joyous Gard* likewise fell victim to the cutters torch after being made available to the scrap metal industry in October 1966.

Traditionally, on northbound inter-regional trains, Southern Region locomotives gave way to their Western Region counterparts at Oxford and vice-versa in the reverse direction. This arrangement ended when Oxford shed was closed to the iron horse at the beginning of 1966, and while the 'Pines Express' to and from Manchester was handed over to diesel traction the daily service between Poole and York was then rostered for a LMS Stanier class 5MT 4-6-0 south of Banbury. After whiling away the night on Bournemouth shed, having had charge of the previous day's southbound working, No 44780 cautiously draws the morning Poole to York service along the up platform road at Eastleigh on 24 May 1966, most of the stock being Mk1s. At the time Crewe Works-built No 44780 was based at the ex-GWR depot at Tyseley (Birmingham) which had been administered by the London Midland Region since September 1963. During its twenty-one-year career, starting at Wakefield shed in July 1947, No 44780 was reallocated on no less than 16 occasions, its longest stay being at Huddersfield where it resided for over eight years. This unusual 'Black 5' diagram ceased the following September. Perhaps it should also be mentioned that when in town Bournemouth shed were not averse to occasionally 'borrowing' these foreigners, particularly on Sundays when there was no York service, and sending them on a trip to London and back during the layover time.

Locally-based Maunsell U class 2-6-0 No 31791 leads a long train of freight wagons through Eastleigh (the station is visible beyond the signal box) as it makes its way towards the docks at Southampton on 4 September 1962. The Mogul had a power classification of 4P3F. The Southern Railway bequeathed 50 of the class to British Railways in 1948, including 20 that had started life as K class 2-6-4Ts which had all been named after rivers. Except for the pioneer of the 2-6-4Ts, No 790 *River Avon*, which first appeared in 1917, the 'Rivers' as such had a very short existence, the other 19 only surfacing from Ashford Works in 1925, including No 31791 (formerly No 791 *River Adur*). By the end of 1928 all 20 were running as 2-6-0s. No 31791 survived at Guildford shed, along with its sister No 31639, until June 1966 when the class was rendered extinct on BR. Four of the earlier withdrawals from 1964 have been preserved, including No 31806, former K class 2-6-4T No 806 *River Torridge*.

On the same day, closely watched by young and old alike from the vantage point near the bottom of Campbell Road, 'West Country' Pacific No 34102 *Lapford* heads south through Eastleigh. Over the years countless numbers of young men (and many not so young) became very familiar with the route from the station along Southampton Road and over the bridge on which the author is standing, as they walked expectantly towards the locomotive works entrance on the left, or continued a little further to the shed gates on the opposite side of the road. Behind and to the right of the train are the carriage works, founded first in 1891. No 34102 first left Eastleigh Works in March 1950, one of only six light Pacifics to be built there, the rest being put together at Brighton. The name of the small Devon village of Lapford, on the ex-LSWR Exeter to Barnstaple line, was conferred on the engine before it left the workshops. When new it was allocated to Stewarts Lane depot in London, where it remained until February 1958 when it was moved to Bournemouth. It was at Eastleigh from September 1964 and by the time it was disposed of in the summer of 1967 had completed 593,438 miles. It was dismembered the following year by J Buttigieg's of Newport, Monmouthshire, who were responsible for the destruction of 19 of the 'West Country/Battle of Britains' together with six 'Merchant Navies', only the nearby John Cashmore's yard handling more of the defunct Bulleid Pacifics.

Passing the same spot where *Lapford* was seen in September 1962, but photographed from the other side of the main line on 24 May 1966, is Doncaster Works 1955-built BR Standard class 5MT 4-6-0 No 73115 *King Pellinore* with an Eastleigh to Southampton Docks transfer freight. The name had earlier been affixed to the side of 'King Arthur' class 4-6-0 No 30738 (1919–1958), No 73115 being decorated with the name of the legendary King of Listinoise in February 1960. The tender is not its original for when new Nos 73110 to 73119 were attached to Type BR1F flush-sided tenders which could accommodate up to 5,625 gallons of water. Here No 73115 is being led by one of the smaller variety of flush-sided tenders with a maximum water capacity of 4,725 gallons. More modern traction is represented by two Sulzer-engined Birmingham RC&W Type 3 (later class 33) Bo-Bo diesel-electric locomotives, while a rather ancient looking departmental carriage, No DS79212, edges into the frame on the left.

The LSWR opened the motive power depot at Eastleigh in 1903 to serve the Southampton area. It was a large double-ended shed with 15 through roads, BR coding it 71A until September 1963 when it became 70D. In 1959 the depot was responsible for 111 steam locomotives and it still had over 100 on its books in 1965. A mixed assortment of power was on view on 5 September 1961, the line on the left awaiting a call to the works comprised (nearest the camera) Adams class O2 0-4-4T No 30183 built back in 1890 (withdrawn after examination at the works), BR Standard class 3MT 2-6-2T No 82014, Maunsell class Q 0-6-0 No 30530, BR Standard class 4MT 2-6-0 No 76009, ex-GWR Collett 0-6-0PT No 4610 (then based at Feltham on the Southern), Bulleid class Q1 0-6-0 No 33024, BR Standard class 4MT 2-6-4T No 80040 and 'King Arthur' class 4-6-0 No 30793 *Sir Ontzlake*.

Twelve months later, on 4 September 1962 (a Tuesday), 94 engines were on shed of 27 different classes. Amongst the veterans on display were Stroudley London, Brighton and South Coast Railway 'Terrier' class A1X 0-6-0T No 32646 of 1876 vintage, Drummond LSWR class T9 4-4-0 No 30120, looking quite resplendent in its pre-Grouping livery as No 120, and the diminutive Adams LSWR class B4 0-4-0T No 30096 designed for dock and yard shunting, the latter two both constructed at Nine Elms in 1899 and 1893 respectively. Happily, all three are still extant, No 32646 back on the Isle of Wight as No W8 *Freshwater* where it served from 1913, initially as Freshwater, Yarmouth and Newport Railway No 2, before returning to the mainland in 1949, while both Nos 30096 and 30120 are on the Bluebell Railway at Sheffield Park in East Sussex. On the same day a further 36 steam locomotives were at the nearby works, including engines of three classes not represented at the shed.

In 1946 the Southern Railway purchased 15 ex-USA Army Transportation Corps 0-6-0Ts specifically for use at Southampton Docks, these having been part of a large batch imported a few years earlier to assist the war effort both at home and in Europe. One was cannibalised as a source of spare parts with the 14 added to stock being numbered 61–74 and officially designated the USA class. As BR Nos 30061–30074 they continued to have charge of the shunting work at the docks until diesels began to take over in 1962. No 30064, built in 1943 by the Vulcan Iron Works at Wilkes-Barre, Pennsylvania, and with its overseas pedigree very evident, stands outside the shed doors at Eastleigh alongside a tender belonging to a Bulleid Pacific on 24 May 1966. In contrast to the visit in September 1962, as detailed in the previous caption, that day only 30 steam locomotives were recorded, including nine which had already been deleted from the active list. Ten classes were represented. Just two of the locomotives were aged over twenty-five years, although both were among those recently withdrawn, U class 2-6-0 No 31803 dating from 1928 and N class 2-6-0 No 31411 of 1933. Today, in company with two of the engines seen in the photograph opposite, No 30064 is also resident on the Bluebell Railway.

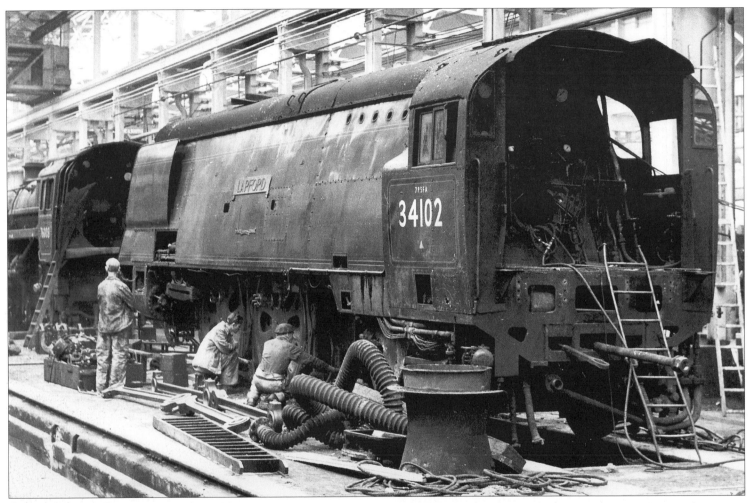

At the end of the nineteenth century the LSWR realised its locomotive workshop facilities at Nine Elms were fast becoming inadequate and the decision was taken to build a new factory at Eastleigh, although it was not finally completed until 1910. In the erecting shop on 24 May 1966, with the motion already having been dismantled, fitters are at work on 'West Country' No 34102 *Lapford*, which was undergoing a Light Casual during a visit to its birthplace. On the left is BR Standard class 4MT 2-6-0 No 76008. Indicative of the rundown of steam, only nine locomotives still itemised on the BR stock list were present for attention that day, including six 'WC/BBs', one 'Merchant Navy' No 35014 *Nederland Line* and two Standard 4MT 2-6-0s. They were complemented by three engines destined for preservation, Drummond M7 class 0-4-4T No 30053, Maunsell 'Schools' class 4-4-0 No 30926 *Repton* and Churchward ex-GWR 2-8-0 No 2818. The works officially closed at the end of March 2006, having been owned by Alstom in its latter days. Fittingly, the last engine to leave the site a few months later (having been allowed a little more time to enable work to be finished ready for another stint of main line running) was former Southern Railway Maunsell 'Lord Nelson' class 4-6-0 No 850 *Lord Nelson*.

As it runs through the suburbs of Southampton bunker-first, BR Standard class 4MT 2-6-4T No 80083 prepares to halt at St Denys with a down local stopping train on a rather wet 24 May 1966. No 80083 was built for the London Midland Region at Brighton during the spring of 1954, being allocated to Bletchley, Rugby and Neasden sheds before an inter-regional transfer within the capital took it to Bricklayers Arms on the Southern in December 1959. From June 1962 it was on the register of Eastleigh shed, where its active days were concluded three months after this photograph was taken in August 1966.

Again on 24 May 1966, Eastleigh-based 'West Country' No 34009 *Lyme Regis* hastens past the imposing signal gantry at the south end of St Denys station with an express bound for Waterloo. The tracks veering off to the left lead to Portsmouth and the coast line to Brighton. The locomotive's nameplates were ceremoniously unveiled on 27 August 1946 (almost a year after it had entered traffic) at Axminster, the junction station on the Salisbury to Exeter main line for the coastal resort of Lyme Regis, the Pacific being far too large to travel down the sharply-curved branch. Incidentally, for many years the Lyme Regis branch was the preserve of the last three surviving Adams LSWR class 0415 4-4-2Ts Nos 30582–4 which turned the scales at 55 tons 2cwt, as against the 86 tons 0cwt of the 'WC/BBs' in their original condition. After rebuilding the weight of the latter increased slightly to 90 tons 1 cwt.

Later the same afternoon, with the tidal River Itchen on the left, double-chimney BR Standard class 4MT 4-6-0 No 75075 shunts the extensive Bevois Park sidings, just to the south of St Denys station. Outshopped from Swindon Works with a single chimney in November 1955 (the double-chimney and blastpipe arrangement was fitted at Eastleigh in September 1961), No 75075 was always a Southern Region engine, being maintained over the years at Exmouth Junction, Basingstoke, Three Bridges, Stewarts Lane and Norwood Junction sheds, before what proved to be its final move to Eastleigh in December 1963. It appeared on a number of occasions during the last week of Southern steam, culminating with the 18.51 Bournemouth to Woking service on Friday 7 July 1967. It met its end a few months later in the yard of A King and Son at Norwich – perhaps the furthest it ever strayed off Southern territory.

About to plunge into the Stygian gloom of Southampton Tunnel, shortly after leaving Southampton Central with a northbound inter-regional train (the leading brake side-corridor carriage No W1633W is a Western Region example), is rebuilt 'West Country' Pacific No 34016 *Bodmin* on 7 September 1962. At Basingstoke the consist will diverge onto ex-Great Western Railway tracks and head towards Reading and Oxford, where *Bodmin* will be relieved, probably by a former GWR 'Hall' or 'Grange' class for the onward trek north. In its air-smoothed condition *Bodmin* was always an Exmouth Junction engine, travelling to the Cornish town for an official naming ceremony by the Mayor on 28 August 1946. The locomotive also carried the county coat of arms featuring a series of bezants. However, after it was rebuilt in April 1958 *Bodmin* was redeployed to Ramsgate shed on the Kent coast, about as far away as possible from its former West Country haunts. In June of the following year, on completion of Stage 1 of the Kent coast electrification scheme, *Bodmin* was moved to Bricklayers Arms pending completion of Stage 2 in the summer of 1961, whereupon it was transferred to Eastleigh. It was to last only another three years in BR service for in June 1964 it was withdrawn, the second of the rebuilds to suffer this fate after No 34028 *Eddystone* the previous month. It was then that fortune smiled on *Bodmin* insomuch that it was bought by Woodham Bros of Barry, scrap dealers who tended to store rather than dismantle most of their locomotive acquisitions. Thus after slowly decaying in the salty sea air that pervaded their South Wales yard for over seven and a half years it was repurchased for preservation in July 1972. Since then it has given many years of excellent service between Alresford and Alton on the Mid-Hants Railway, and on a number of main line specials.

'Merchant Navy' class 4-6-2 No 35028 *Clan Line* coasts into Southampton Central, known as Southampton West until July 1935, with a Waterloo to Bournemouth and Weymouth train on a damp 24 May 1966. The entrance to Southampton Tunnel can be seen in the background above the rear carriages. With neither the LSWR nor their successors laying any water troughs there was a necessity for all engines on long-distance services to take water at Southampton during the station stop. *Clan Line* entered traffic from Eastleigh Works in December 1948 and was the last of the class to be rebuilt there in October 1959. Almost immediately after its withdrawal in July 1967 the Merchant Navy Locomotive Preservation Society handed over a cheque to BR to ensure its survival. Under their stewardship it returned to the main line in 1974 and since then has added many more miles to the 794,391 recorded while in the care of the BR depots at Bournemouth, Dover, Stewarts Lane, Nine Elms, Weymouth and then Nine Elms again for its final three months in state ownership.

On the same day, 'West Country' No 34006 *Bude* trundles slowly through Southampton with a mixed assortment of parcels vans. The position of the two white discs mounted on the front lamp brackets indicates *Bude* was on its way back to Salisbury, its home base after September 1964. Previously it was at Nine Elms from April 1951 and before that at Exmouth Junction. Notice the six electric lamps which were illuminated as appropriate during the hours of darkness to advertise the headcode – the Southern used over 30 different combinations of one, two or three discs or lamps in respect of its various routes. No 34006 took its name from the north Cornwall coastal town of Bude, travelling there for the usual ceremony on 1 November 1945. Bude was reached by a former LSWR branch from Halwill Junction, completed in 1898, although the town lost its train service when the line closed on 3 October 1966. When named the Pacific bore the county coat of arms, but the plaques were later changed to the one seen here below the name following Bude-Stratton UDC being granted its own heraldic device by the College of Arms in September 1947. In 1948 *Bude* participated in the BR Locomotive Exchange trials and its performance was analysed in detail over the former Great Central Railway Manchester London Road to Marylebone route and the ex-GWR Bristol to Plymouth line. *Bude* was condemned in March 1967 after amassing a grand total of 1,099,338 miles, the highest recorded by a light Pacific. Two others, Nos 34001 *Exeter* and 34002 *Salisbury*, also exceeded one million miles.

Observed from the bridge depicted in the previous illustration, Brighton-based 'Battle of Britain' No 34057 *Biggin Hill* rolls into Southampton with a Plymouth to Brighton service on the sunny afternoon of 7 September 1962. The 4-6-2 had taken over the train at Salisbury, after earlier in the day working the corresponding morning service in the opposite direction as far as the cathedral city. Beyond the signal gantry governing movements in the down direction is an ocean liner berthed in Southampton Western Docks, by the River Test, along with numerous dockside cranes. The brick-built signal box, in view above the leading two carriages, was manned from June 1935 until November 1981, whereupon the power box at

Eastleigh gained control of the area. During its twenty-year life, *Biggin Hill*, after starting out from Stewarts Lane depot in London in March 1947 was reallocated on ten subsequent occasions to sheds as far apart as Dover and Exmouth Junction. Its most unusual posting was that to Stratford (London) on the Eastern Region in May 1951, together with Nos 34039 *Boscastle* and 34065 *Hurricane*, to operate East Anglian services out of Liverpool Street, the BR Board deeming the Southern to have a surfeit of Pacifics at this time. They were joined in November by Nos 34076 *41 Squadron* and 34089 *602 Squadron* but by June 1952 they were all back on the Southern. No 34057 finished its days at Salisbury from September 1963.

In the heart of the New Forest, 'West Country' 4-6-2 No 34100 *Appledore* hauls the 13.30 Waterloo to Weymouth service over the level crossing at Brockenhurst, the junction station for the Lymington branch, on 22 October 1966. During torrential downpours such as this the canopy sheltering the footpath leading to the down-side station entrance, visible to the left of the large station nameboard, was most welcome.

Despite being named after the small village on the north Devon coast near Bideford, *Appledore* spent the first fourteen years of its life much further east on attachment to the sheds at Ramsgate, Stewarts Lane and Brighton, much nearer to the village of the same name on the Ashford to Hastings line in Kent, before moving to Salisbury in September 1963. The engine lost its air-smoothed casing in September 1960.

Later that same day, shortly after returning from a trip to Lymington, BR Standard class 4MT 2-6-4T No 80134 has its 2,000 gallon-capacity side tanks replenished at the east end of Brockenhurst station. The flat-roofed signal box dating from November 1964 can be glimpsed behind the water crane. No 80134 led a somewhat nomadic life. Constructed at Brighton Works during the spring of 1956, it was the Eastern Region (the former London, Tilbury and Southend Railway depots at Plaistow and Tilbury) and the Western Region (Swansea East Dock and Llanelly sheds in South Wales) that benefited from its presence before it eventually arrived back on the Southern, initially at Feltham, in July 1964. The next month it was reallocated to Bournemouth, where it remained until discarded by BR in July 1967.

With the conductor rail already in position by both running lines, Eastleigh-allocated BR Standard class 4MT 2-6-4T No 80016 nears Lymington Junction, one-mile west of Brockenhurst, with a stopping train bound for Bournemouth on 20 October 1966. The branch to Lymington was opened in July 1858. Almost thirty years later, in March 1888, it became a three-way junction when the new direct line from Christchurch was connected to the 'old' road from the west at this location. Today the two surviving routes no longer converge here (the Ringwood line having closed to both passengers and goods on 4 May 1964) for the Lymington branch trains now use a dedicated track positioned on the south side of the down Bournemouth line, access to which is gained at Brockenhurst. No 80016 was manufactured at Brighton Works in September 1951 and subsequently spent all its days on the Southern Region, alternating between Tunbridge Wells West and Brighton sheds before moving to Eastleigh in June 1964 for its last three years of activity.

BR Standard 2-6-4T No 80019 from Bournemouth shed is ready to leave Lymington Pier with a train for Brockenhurst on 24 October 1966. The single white disc carried just above the centre of the buffer beam was the headcode used by trains serving Lymington. On the right is the car ferry *Farringford*, a diesel-electric paddler, on the connecting ferry service to Yarmouth, Isle of Wight. The branch was the last on BR to be worked by steam, the finale occurring on Sunday 2 April 1967 when specially smartened up Ivatt class 2MT 2-6-2T No 41312 performed the last rites.

It bore a suitable home-made headboard, as had the branch engines during the previous week, 'The Last Steam Branch 1967'. The next day, as an interim measure pending the inauguration of electric traction the following June, diesel units took charge of the branch operating on a 'one engine in steam' principle. A final steam special, the Locomotive Club of Great Britain-sponsored 'Hampshire Branch Lines Rail Tour', ventured down the branch on Sunday 9 April hauled by 4MT 2-6-4T No 80151 tailed by 2MT 2-6-2T No 41320.

Sadly, the Lymington to Yarmouth ferry has had no corresponding rail link near its island terminal since the Freshwater to Yarmouth and Newport line closed back in September 1953. In fact, since 18 April 1966 the only line to have remained open for passengers on the Isle of Wight is that between Ryde Pier Head and Shanklin. During the nineteenth century a number of companies administered the island's rail network, although it was left to the London and South Western and the London, Brighton and South Coast railways to open the Ryde Pier Head to Ryde St John's Road section as a joint venture in 1880 in order to ensure convenient connections with the railway-owned ferries plying across the Spithead from Portsmouth. Here, on

25 May 1966, class O2 0-4-4T No W24 *Calbourne*, built at Nine Elms by the LSWR in 1891, hauls a rake of vintage non-corridor stock along the half mile-long pier towards Ryde Esplanade while forming the 17.19 Ryde Pier Head to Shanklin service. One of the BR-owned Sealink ferries can be seen berthed on the right. A Drewry diesel-powered railcar, one of two which shuttled back and forth along the pier tramway between the Pier Head and Esplanade stations, is visible on the left. The tramway closed in January 1969. *Calbourne* is now the only O2 still in existence. It is preserved, appropriately, on the Isle of Wight Steam Railway which operates between Smallbrook Junction and Wootton, a line once owned by the Isle of Wight Central Railway.

During the last few years of Wight steam all services were monopolised by a batch of Adams LSWR class O2 0-4-4Ts built at Nine Elms from 1889, the last in 1892. In total 23 were shipped from the mainland between 1923 and 1949, adapted with Westinghouse air braking equipment and from 1932 with larger coal bunkers. The locomotive stock on the island was always numbered in a separate series to those on the other side of The Solent and from 1928, in common with long-standing practice, the O2s also received names with an island connection. In this scene septuagenarian No W14 *Fishbourne* arrives bunker first at Ryde St John's Road while returning to the Pier Head with the 13.55 from Shanklin on 25 May 1966. On the right No W35 *Freshwater* rests in the shed yard. The signal box was equipped with a 40-lever frame with which to control the movements through the station, on and off the adjacent shed as well as the works on the opposite side of the line. It was erected here in 1928 after seeing previous use at Waterloo East on the ex-South Eastern and Chatham Railway.

Following the closure of Newport shed (code 70G) in November 1957, the two-road shed at Ryde (70H) assumed sole responsibility for the island's motive power needs. Shortly after returning to the shed from a stint of duty on the Shanklin service, the driver of No W31 *Chale* cleans the accumulated ash from the smokebox while No W20 *Shanklin* waits alongside, again on 25 May 1966. Note the running numbers stencilled on the right-hand side of the buffer beams. They had a power classification of 0P. Between the two engines can be seen the rather basic coal stage, somewhat of a contrast to the facilities available at Nine Elms (see page 11).

On the same day as the previous picture, four O2s are viewed from inside the shed building. Between Nos W20 *Shanklin* (left) and W31 *Chale* (right) are W29 *Alverstone* and W26 *Whitwell*, the latter pair having just been withdrawn from service. From this angle the steam-driven Westinghouse air brake pumps and the associated reservoirs fixed on top of the side tanks are clearly evident, as are the extended coal bunkers which doubled their original capacity to three tons. As can be discerned by the markings on the engines, by this date the nameplates had been removed from the side tanks, as had the small oval number plates previously affixed to the back of the bunkers.

With the lofty 32-lever signal box overlooking the scene, No W20 *Shanklin* pulls away from Sandown with the 16.19 from Ryde Pier Head to Shanklin on 25 May 1966. The outer face of the up platform on the left was once frequented by trains to Cowes via Merstone and Newport. This service ceased on 6 February 1956. No W20, formerly LSWR No 211, was constructed at Nine Elms in 1892 and was one of the two O2s imported to the island by the Southern Railway in 1923, the other being No W19 *Osborne* which was withdrawn in November 1955. No W20 remained in service until the end of the year and was dismantled on the island at Newport during May 1967.

By May 1966 Shanklin was the limit of the passenger service from Ryde, the line on to Ventnor having closed the previous month on 18 April. Having arrived a little earlier with the 11.19 from Ryde Pier Head on 25 May of that year, 76 years old No W31 *Chale*, having run round its train and propelled the coaches a little way down the line towards Ventnor, pulls them into the up platform ready to form the 11.55 return working to Ryde.

With the ferry beckoning at Ryde Pier Head we take the opportunity of a last look at a class O2 during May 1966. While another train runs into the terminus on the right, the signalman has already raised the semaphore signal at the end of the platform to allow No W31 *Chale* to depart on yet another trip to Shanklin, a 20mph speed restriction having to be observed along the pier. The leading coach, No S4153, is a former London, Brighton and South Coast Railway six-compartment brake third. Part of the signal box governing movements in and out of the station is visible to the right of the locomotive. It had 28 levers and was retained until May 1974. No W31 was constructed at Nine Elms in April 1890 as LSWR No 180. It was transported to the island in May 1927 and later bestowed with the name *Chale*, that of the small village near St Catherine's Point, the southernmost tip of the island. The last BR steam passenger services on the island ran on 31 December 1966, *Chale* being retained along with No W24 *Calbourne* for a few weeks to assist the engineering department prior to the introduction of the electric trains on 20 March 1967.

Returning to the mainland we resume our journey through the New Forest towards Bournemouth with a view of rebuilt 'West Country' Pacific No 34013 *Okehampton* climbing the 1-in-103 gradient away from Lymington Junction with the 13.30 Waterloo to Weymouth service on 25 October 1966. In the distance, beyond the road on the left, is the embankment which formerly carried the original LSWR route to the west via Ringwood and Wimborne. Initially *Okehampton* was stationed in the West Country at Exmouth Junction and Plymouth Friary sheds, but after shedding its air-smoothed casing in October 1957 it was relocated to Bricklayers Arms and then Brighton, before Salisbury became its home from September 1963.

With the Lymington Junction distant signal in the off position, indicating a clear road ahead at least as far as Brockenhurst, the last 'Merchant Navy' to roll off the assembly lines at Eastleigh in April 1949, Weymouth-based No 35030 *Elder Dempster Lines*, hurries downgrade with the up 'Bournemouth Belle' Pullman service en route back to the capital on 19 October 1966. The track has already been upgraded and the third rail put in position for the forthcoming electric service but, unfortunately, when the new timetable was inaugurated the following July there was no place for this luxurious train. It last ran on Sunday 9 July 1967, regrettably, to the disappointment of many, behind Brush Type 4 diesel-electric No D1924 (later No 47247), although it had been hauled by steam on a couple of occasions during the previous week.

The next day BR Standard class 5MT 4-6-0 No 73037 is pictured at the same location with a train from Waterloo heading for Bournemouth. The Lymington Junction up distant signal is just visible to the left of the rear carriages. The engine's front number plate has been removed, although its identity has been stencilled on the buffer beam, albeit on this occasion hardly decipherable under an accumulation of grime. When No 73037 emerged from Derby Works in September 1953 it was provisionally intended for Polmadie shed in Glasgow, but before it could travel north to Scotland it was diverted to the Western Region depot at Shrewsbury. It only became the responsibility of the Southern Region in April 1965 when it was relocated from Oxford to Eastleigh, before moving to Guildford the next month. By June 1966 it was at Nine Elms. Unlike some of its counterparts originally supplied to the Southern, which had slightly larger, high-sided tenders (see pages 28 and 62), No 73037 was attached to a Type BR1 inset 4,250 gallon, seven ton coal capacity tender. It remained active until the very last week of steam in the south in July 1967.

Rebuilt 'West Country' 4-6-2 No 34040 *Crewkerne* passes Sway, 95½ miles into its journey with the Saturdays Only 12.35 from Waterloo to Bournemouth, on a dismal 22 October 1966. Even though it will be some weeks before the third rails in the area are energised, a sign has already been erected near the end of the up platform warning "Danger Don't Touch Conductor Rails". Note, too, the painted brickwork on the bridge behind the signal to aid sighting of the semaphore by drivers of up trains, and while it is now some forty years since the signal was dismantled, the white paint (albeit a little faded) remains visible to this day. The engine spent the first two years of its life from September 1946 based at Stewarts Lane shed as No 21C140. On 20 October 1948, five days after receiving its BR identity of 34040, it travelled specially to its adopted town in Somerset, on the ex-LSWR main line between Yeovil Junction (No 34004 took the name *Yeovil*) and Axminster (No 34018), where the Chairman of Crewkerne Urban District Council with due ceremony officially made known the name. *Crewkerne* was a Bournemouth engine from June 1956, having run just over 500,000 miles by the time it was rebuilt in October 1960. Another 269,000 were added before it was withdrawn in July 1967.

On the same day the signalman at Sway accepts the single line token from the fireman on BR Standard class 4MT 2-6-0 No 76009 as it prepares to stop with the three-coach 13.52 Bournemouth to Southampton service. Single line working was temporarily in force over the up line between here and New Milton to allow the permanent way department unhindered access to the down line while relaying the track with long-welded rails and installing the conductor rail. The Mogul was despatched new from Horwich Works in Lancashire to the Southern Region in February 1953. During its lifetime it had three separate stints working from Eastleigh shed, interspersed with short periods at Redhill, Yeovil Town and Salisbury, prior to finishing its career at Bournemouth from October 1965. Its fire was last lit in July 1967.

At New Milton on 25 October 1966, 'West Country' Pacific No 34015 *Exmouth*, running 'wrong line', nears the end of the three-mile single line section from Sway with a down goods train. The signal box (closed February 1967), situated just off the far end of the up platform is hidden from sight by the footbridge. The main station building, behind the footbridge, was completed by the LSWR in 1886, two years ahead of services commencing along the route. Today, displayed on the walls of the booking hall and the small waiting room, by way of a local initiative, are a fine selection of railway photographs and other artifacts from past eras. Appropriately, when new in November 1945, the engine was allocated to Exmouth Junction shed, where it remained, except for a brief interlude at Salisbury during February/March 1951, until September 1964 when it returned to Salisbury on a permanent basis. It ran 903,245 miles before its withdrawal notice was issued on 16 April 1967.

While a porter pushes a trolley along the platform at New Milton, passengers awaiting the 10.43 Southampton to Bournemouth service keenly observe its approach 'wrong line' behind Standard class 4MT 2-6-4T No 80085 on 19 October 1966. The station nameboard by the bike shed on the opposite platform (still well-used today) reads "New Milton for Milford-on-Sea and Barton-on-Sea". A vintage LSWR sign near the bottom of the footbridge steps advises "Passengers Must Cross Line By Bridge". The castellated building on the right is a local water authority pumping station. No 80085 was officially transferred to the Southern from the London Midland Region in December 1959 following an agreement between the two regions, whereby the former accepted 34 Standard 4MT 2-6-4Ts in exchange for a like number of LMS-designed Fairburn 2-6-4Ts which moved in the opposite direction, although it took a few weeks to effect all the moves. In contrast to its time on the LMR, where it had spent almost all its five and a half years at Bletchley shed (it had one month at Rugby), once south of the Thames the locomotive never seemed to have time to put any roots down before it was once more being moved on to a new home. In fact, the relevant engine history card details its time at no less than eight Southern sheds starting with Bricklayers Arms, followed by Ashford, Tonbridge, Stewarts Lane, Brighton, Redhill, Feltham and finally Nine Elms from October 1966.

The previous day the 10.43 from Southampton was in the hands of sister Standard 2-6-4T No 80139 from Eastleigh shed, seen here at Hinton Admiral where but a solitary figure is in evidence under the canopy on the right. Worthy of note are the 1886-constructed station building on the left, the decorative stanchion brackets supporting the canopies, the corrugated-iron shed and the body from an old goods van providing some additional storage space on the up platform. No 80139 arrived on the Southern at the end of 1959 as part of the large scale swap of Standard and Fairburn 2-6-4Ts with the London Midland Region referred to in the previous caption. This was the second inter-regional decision to affect No 80139, for earlier, in February 1958, when it was based at the ex-Great Central Railway shed at Neasden in north-west London, it had been transferred from Eastern Region to LMR control as part of a wider regional restructuring scheme. Thus in the 1960s No 80139 found itself carrying the shed code plates for Tunbridge Wells West (75F), Brighton (75A), Redhill (75B) and lastly that of Eastleigh (70D). After withdrawal from capital stock in July 1967, along with classmates Nos 80085 seen overleaf at New Milton, 80134 sighted at Brockenhurst (page 41) and 80016 near Lymington Junction (page 42), No 80139 was sold to Bird's of Risca, near Newport, where during the first two months of 1968 they were all reduced to more manageable fragments of metal for resale to the steel industry.

With its wheels shrouded in steam, rebuilt 'Battle of Britain' Pacific No 34052 *Lord Dowding* blasts away from Christchurch with a train bound for London on the morning of 22 October 1966. The train is passing the former 1888-installed junction with the earlier route to London via Ringwood, the latter having been deprived of passenger trains since September 1935. Although the engine had taken up its duties at the end of 1946 as No 21C152, it was not named until 11 September 1947 when retired Air Chief Marshal Lord Dowding pulled the curtain back to reveal his name and private crest during a ceremony at Waterloo station. A few minutes earlier he had performed a similar duty in respect of No 21C151 (34051) *Winston Churchill*, while No 21C164 (34064) was named *Fighter Command* on the same occasion. During the formal proceedings a number of Southern Railway employees who had served in the Royal Air Force formed a Guard of Honour on the platform. After rebuilding in September 1958 the nameplates and plaques were mounted on the running plate, the crest then being placed above rather than below the name. When the engine was withdrawn in July 1967 it had accumulated 936,502 miles.

Looking in exemplary condition, rebuilt 'Battle of Britain' Pacific No 34077 *603 Squadron* emerges from under Holdenhurst Road and into Bournemouth Central station, 108 miles from Waterloo, on Sunday 3 September 1961. In July 1885 the station replaced the town's earlier East terminus (on the opposite side of the road) which was then relegated to a goods depot. The new station similarly bore the suffix East until May 1899 when it became known as Central. Standing proud behind the bridge, overlooking both sites, is the appropriately titled South Western Hotel (now a nightclub). Named without ceremony after one of the RAF squadrons that helped defend the air space over south-east England during the Battle of Britain in 1940, No 34077 was one of 40 Light Pacifics to enter service after Britain's railways had been vested in the state at the beginning of 1948, arriving new at Ramsgate shed in July of that year. After coming under the jurisdiction of the shed foreman at Stewarts Lane for most of 1949, it was returned to Ramsgate where it stayed until the beginning of 1958, went it went back to Stewarts Lane. While based at the latter it was rebuilt in July 1960, before being transferred to Nine Elms in May 1961, Feltham in September 1964 and finally Eastleigh in November 1964. It was marked for scrap on 26 March 1967.

Despite having only a few more steaming days left before its fire was extinguished for the last time, Maunsell 4-cylinder 'Lord Nelson' class 4-6-0 No 30857 *Lord Howe* confidently sets out from Bournemouth Central with the 10.25 Poole to Bradford service on Saturday 8 September 1962. The 'Nelson' hauled the train as far as Oxford. When the pioneer of the class No 850 *Lord Nelson* made its début at Eastleigh Works in August 1926, with a tractive effort of 33,510lbs, it was rightly hailed as the most powerful express locomotive in Britain. Fifteen similar engines were constructed between May 1928 and November 1929, *Lord Howe* in December 1928. At the turn of the decade into the 1960s the class was concentrated at Eastleigh where the youngest, No 30865 *Sir John Hawkins*, was condemned in May 1961. By October 1962 the rest had been cast aside. Only one, No 850 *Lord Nelson*, has been preserved (see page 32).

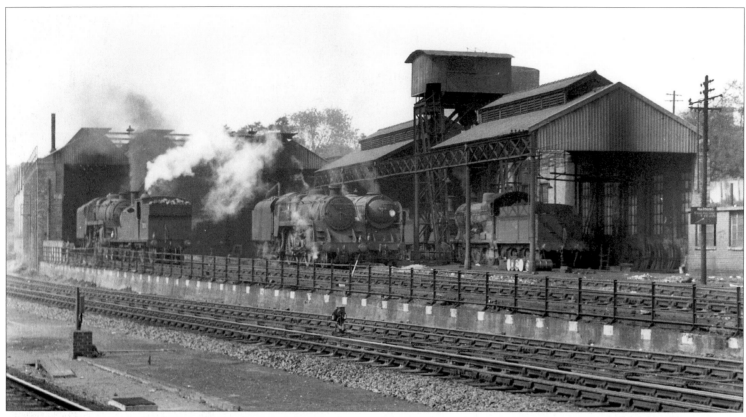

Bournemouth shed was on a rather constricted site, rail access being gained via a connection close to the west end of the up platform. Only four roads were available for storage and preparation needs, plus an additional short length for minor repair work. In BR days the shed was coded 71B, that is until September 1963 when it was amended to 70F. Excessive smoke and noise levels were always a cause for concern due to the close proximity of some domestic properties on the north side of the yard, prominent notices being displayed to remind staff to keep these pollutants to a minimum, not always with success! Despite the difficulties, Bournemouth was an important shed with a sizable allocation, for example in May 1959 60 locomotives displayed 71B shed plates on their smokebox doors, half of them members of the larger, more prestigious classes, including seven 'King Arthur' 4-6-0s, three 'Lord Nelson' 4-6-0s, 13 'West Country' and seven 'Merchant Navy' Pacifics. At the start of 1967 the fleet had been reduced to 21, consisting of six 'West Countrys', five Ivatt LMS class 2MT 2-6-2Ts, five BR Standard class

4MT 2-6-0s and five BR Standard class 4MT 2-6-4Ts. The station's 1,760ft-long down platform, extended in 1928 to accommodate two full length trains with a scissors crossover roughly halfway along its length to allow flexibility of operation, effectively doubled as an ideal gallery from which to note the comings and goings at the shed in reasonable comfort in all weather conditions. This scene was observed from the platform on 3 September 1961 with two BR Standard class 5MT 4-6-0s Nos 73112 *Morgan le Fay* (near the running lines on the left) and 73083 *Pendragon*, M7 0-4-4T No 30112 and 'Merchant Navy' 4-6-2 No 35020 *Bibby Line* basking in the sunshine. The repair road, with a 50 ton hoist rising above, is occupied by Q class 0-6-0 No 30539 along with another M7, No 30031, which was in fact the former No 30128, the pair having exchanged identities the previous January (the first No 30031 then being scrapped as No 30128). Once steam had departed from the shed for the last time in July 1967 it was soon demolished in order to make way for a car park.

In addition to the larger passenger classes, Bournemouth shed also provided a home for quite a number of smaller engines, including in 1959 a stud of 16 Drummond LSWR M7 0-4-4Ts and two Adams LSWR class B4 0-4-0Ts. Three years later, on 3 September 1962, M7 No 30379, while on station pilot duty, hauls some empty coaching stock under Beechey Road and past the corrugated side elevation of the shed towards the up platform. All told 105 M7s were built from 1897 – 95 at Nine Elms with the last ten at Eastleigh in 1911 after the LSWR had transferred its workshop facilities to the Hampshire town. During the 1930s the Southern Railway equipped 36 M7s, including No 30379, with Westinghouse air-braking equipment for use on push-pull trains. After giving yeoman service for over fifty-nine years, the dreaded condemnation mark was chalked on the side of No 30379 in October 1963, although 14 of its kind did soldier on into 1964, the last survivors finally bowing out in May of that year. Two M7s have been preserved – No 30053 (one of the last few to be domiciled at Bournemouth in 1964) on the nearby Swanage Railway and No 30245 (as LSWR No 245) at the National Railway Museum in York.

Ancient and modern at Bournemouth on 8 September 1961. On the right M7 0-4-4T No 30379, of 1904 vintage, bides time as 'West Country' class Pacific No 34022 *Exmoor*, dating from 1946 although only from 1957 in its rebuilt form, approaches with a train from Weymouth. No 30379, having just dragged a set of carriages which had arrived from Bournemouth West into the siding by the shed, was awaiting the arrival of the Weymouth train, whereupon the M7 shunted its stock onto the rear, the two portions then forming a combined service through to Waterloo. Today Bournemouth's citizens enjoy a fast, frequent service to London provided by electric multiple-units, while many parts of the Midlands, the north of England and Scotland can be accessed direct by an hourly service of Voyager diesel units. Further, in 2000 the station benefited from a £7m restoration and refurbishment scheme, including replacement of the glazing in the overall roof, much of which had been missing for many years (see page 61). Thus the 1885 buildings now look in pristine condition. Even so, despite these obvious improvements, if only one could step back in time now and again and relive the days of the 1950s and 1960s when Bulleid Pacifics and other ex-Southern Railway classes, along with some of the BR Standards, held sway along the former LSWR tracks up to London. They were truly memorable times.